Usability Testing
for Library Web Sites

A Hands-On Guide

 ELAINA NORLIN CM! WINTERS

AMERICAN LIBRARY ASSOCIATION
Chicago and London
2002

Cover and text design: Dianne M. Rooney

Composition in Minion and ITC Officina Sans using QuarkXpress 4.1 for the Macintosh by the dotted i

Printed on 60-pound white offset, a pH-neutral stock, and bound in 10-point cover stock by McNaughton & Gunn

The paper used in this publication meets the minimum requirements of American National Standard for Information Sciences—Permanence of Paper for Printed Library Materials, ANSI Z39.48-1992.♾

Library of Congress Cataloging-in-Publication Data

Norlin, Elaina.
    Usability testing for library Web sites : a hands-on guide / Elaina Norlin, CM! Winters.
        p.   cm.
    Includes index.
    ISBN 0-8389-3511-7 (alk. paper)
    1. Library Web sites—Testing.   2. User interfaces (Computer systems)— Testing.   3. Web sites—Design.   I. Title: Usability testing for library Web sites. II. Winters, CM!   III. Title.
    Z674.75.W67 N67 2001
    020'.285'5276—dc21

                                                    2001033817

Printed in the United States of America.

06 05 04 03 02   5 4 3 2 1

CONTENTS

FIGURES

PREFACE

People acquire information from many sources other than libraries. For example, Barnes & Noble, Borders, and Amazon .com sell and distribute books, videos, and CDs and compete for the time and attention of our library's customers. Barnes & Noble also provides children's programming and Internet-related classes for families. These competitors for our library's customers can afford to spend an enormous amount of money creating in-depth, user-friendly Web sites that customers access on a daily basis. Their Web sites are often state-of-the-art, with phenomenal graphics and interactivity that help attract and maintain new clientele. In addition, these competitors often have money and resources to do in-depth usability studies to find out if customers are easily navigating their Web sites and finding information effectively.

Although the main purpose of these competitors' Web sites is to ultimately sell products and services, many of today's library customers are used to slick advertising, beautiful graphics, and very little text. Most libraries do not have enough money or resources to contract with consultants or companies to create extensive and exciting Web sites. However, all libraries can make sure that their library interfaces are easy to navigate, are understandable, and have instructions that make all customers—those who come into the library and those who do not—as self-sufficient as possible.

Today, the typical library has a Web site. At best, the site should provide well-organized information with colorful graphics. The site should be checked periodically to make sure the links are still active. The Web site might also have a "how are we doing?" online survey to solicit comments from its customers. However, the question of the day is Do you know if your library customers are finding the information on your library Web site, or are they giving up in frustration?

The emergence of electronic resources including full-text articles and electronic books and journals makes it even more crucial that you evaluate your library's Web site. As the library continues to acquire more and more electronic resources, organizing them in a way that makes sense becomes essential. Usability testing can help you see where these resources fit logically into the site. It may also suggest that you incorporate multiple formats or organize the library's ever-expanding Web site.

The problem with library Web sites is that librarians often have adopted a "we know best" philosophy when designing them. Librarians commonly organize their Web sites like they organize the library—in a very detailed manner and with an endless amount of information. Librarians also commonly have their own language that they expect all library customers to understand. Words like "catalog" and "indexes" are everyday language to librarians, but to most people these terms can be as foreign as French or Swahili. Most library Web sites need to provide more chances for customer feedback so that customers can be more successful using the sites if librarians are not around to help. Web sites also need to provide more ways to access the same information. Each customer is different—some people prefer visual formats, some enjoy using pull-down menus, some prefer to turn to frequently asked questions. Testing a Web site for usability can help you understand how to eliminate ambiguity and develop a common terminology and language that all Web site users can understand.

Usability Testing for Library Web Sites provides the essentials to get your Web site usability testing project started. The first three chapters serve as a tutorial, providing background information. In chapter 1, you will learn what usability testing is and why it should be part of your entire library's Web site development initiatives. Chapter 2 reiterates Web design recommendations considered fundamental to the development of any "good" Web page. Chapter 3 focuses on how to convince others of the value of library Web site usability testing. Chapters 4 and 5 walk you through the preassessment and application process of usability testing; chapter 6 provides an actual walkthrough of the usability testing process.

If you are a beginner at Web site usability testing, you can start with the history of this testing. If you know what usability testing is but do not know how to get started, chapter 3 will explain how to get buy-in and chapter 4 will help narrow down areas for the usability test. However, if you have been thinking about usability testing and just want to dive in, chapters 5 and 6 give step-by-step instructions on how to conduct the usability test.

ACKNOWLEDGMENTS

We want to thank the people who helped make this book a reality. Writing it would not have been possible without the encouragement and support from colleagues and family and, more importantly, God/dess and the Divine spirits.

We first would like to thank ALA Editions, especially our editor Tarshel Beards, who really helped us through some very difficult times and guided us throughout the entire writing process. We would also like to express gratitude and appreciation to the University of Minnesota Library Residents Program inaugural group, and Patricia Morris.

Elaina would especially like to send a special thank you to her wonderful family and friends, especially Mr. Fay for keeping her grounded. She would also like to thank the University of Arizona Library and especially Access 2000 members for giving her a chance to become a part of a successful Web project team for the University of Arizona Library.

CM! would especially like to extend a warm thanks to her family and friends, especially her incredibly loving husband, J. Johari Palacio, and their newborn, Miles. She would also like to acknowledge the support of the University of Illinois at Chicago Main Library and her Florida State University doctoral committee—Dr. Elfreda A. Chatman, chair, and Drs. Jane Robbins, Robert Blazek, and Victoria MacDonald.

1

Foundations of Usability Testing

Web sites in libraries are now as common as books. Most libraries rely on their Web site to provide service when the library's doors are closed as well as when they are open. These Web sites not only provide information about locale and hours of operation but they also allow users to search online catalogs and charge out resources. At their best, these services are literally as close as a "click of the mouse."

Because practically every library has a Web site, Web design has consequently become the latest addition to the duties and position descriptions of many librarians. Some libraries outsource the development of their Web site, and other libraries rely on the in-house expertise of its personnel. Either way, libraries are challenged with the responsibility of developing a Web site that provides a tremendous amount of information in a noncluttered, easy-to-use way. The responsibility to develop a Web site that is informative and user-friendly is not an easy task. Because there are many resources on *developing* a "good" Web site, this book does not recapitulate those principles. Instead, it focuses on *testing* your Web site to assess its usability. After all, if it is usable, it *is* a good Web site.

THE CONCEPT OF USABILITY TESTING

The International Standards Organization provides an operational definition of usability. It explains that usability establishes the "effectiveness, efficiency, and satisfaction with which a specified set of users can achieve a specified set of tasks in a particular environment." For the purpose of this book, Web site usability testing is defined as a research and development method that involves end users who provide feedback on the Web site design. The end users interact with the Web site by completing a set of real tasks. Empirical data such as the end users' behaviors and expectations are then recorded, analyzed, and ultimately used to make changes or improvements to the Web site. Integration of this iterative design process with the Web site development process will ensure that the site is easy to use, is useful, and increases user satisfaction.

Market Research and Usability Testing

Usability testing is routinely traced back to the realms of marketing, though it has its origins in aircraft design (Kaplan 2000). Usability testing is often a marketing term used when designers collect qualitative and quantitative data about the development of a product. It is a "user-centered design" process that involves the user in the many facets of product development, from initial design to site upgrade. In marketing, the concept of usability testing is commonly referred to as "product usability." Market researchers study the customer's needs and behaviors relative to a specific product. Product usability measures physiological and performance factors as well as the effectiveness of instructions and the usefulness of specific product characteristics. Ultimately, it allows customers to concentrate on the use of the product in a controlled environment. Within this controlled environment, testers observe the user interacting with a product.

Market researchers then set up an experiment in which they can evaluate the use of a product with a sample group (i.e., end users). The sample group is representative of the targeted user population. For example, the product of a library or information service agency would be the library Web site and the sample group would be library users. It is important to note that the target group always consists of the intended users. By incorporating the users, Web developers can uncover problems with the Web site.

Ergonomics and Marketing

Usability testing is also prevalent in the realm of ergonomics. *Ergonomics* is "the study of the efficiency of a person or persons in their work environment," which dates back to World War II. Since its inception, ergonomics has evolved into factors of design and safety. However, in the 1990s the emphasis on ergonomics was the impetus behind what Robert Kaplan (2000) calls "usernomics."

Usernomics integrates ergonomic design and marketing to "produce real-world solutions" in the product and development cycle. The development cycle employs three basic components—product design, usability testing, and marketing (Usernomics 1999).

Kaplan (2000) explained in an electronic interview, "Today, when people talk about ergonomics they usually are referring to making people comfortable and healthy as in chair and desk design. This is really biomechanics." But the advent of marketing and usernomics has increased the popularity of usability testing in software and Web site development. In the computer and Web site research and development industry, usability is advised. Web specialists have begun to popularize the concept of usability testing.

Web Site Design and Usability Testing

As Web sites become pervasive, the need for ongoing evaluation of current Web sites and those under development becomes increasingly evident. Usability testing involves the collection of data about how users actually interact with a product by performing a task in a given environment or work setting. Web site usability testing enables librarians and Web site developers alike to assess the effectiveness of their library's Web design. For example, a "good" Web site is one that can be used with relative ease by the end user whereas a "bad" Web site is one that is not easy to use.

Web site usability testing begins with a frame of mind that puts the end user first. The object of usability testing is to evaluate the Web site from the user's perspective. It is important to enlist usability testing participants who are representative of the population intended to use the Web site and to involve the user in all facets of the design process. The testing focuses on many aspects of a person's interaction with the Web site—ease of learning and use, reduction in errors, and subjective experience.

In addition to user-centered design, instruments such as surveys, questionnaires, focus groups, and observations can be used to assess Web site usability. Each of these has its drawbacks. For example, surveys and questionnaires usually measure only satisfaction. Focus groups engage the user with the product only through the use of a moderator. Although field observation involves the user and the product in the actual environment of use, the environment can serve as a distraction to the assessment of the product being tested. In contrast, Web site usability testing permits concentration on the use of the product through a controlled environment. It requires the undivided attention of the user interacting with the product.

Research Strategies

McGrath (2000) explains four research strategies to evaluate a product such as a Web site:

field strategies

experimental strategies

respondent strategies

theoretical strategies

In a field strategy, the Web site is observed in lieu of a field experiment or field study such as beta testing. A Web site evaluated in light of an experimental strategy would require controlling certain conditions of the study. In the respondent strategy, users' opinions are documented via a survey, a questionnaire, or an interview. A Web site evaluated using a theoretical strategy would involve computer simulation, such as a cognitive walkthrough (i.e., storyboard).

Web site usability testing falls under the category of experimental strategy, because it involves observing a user in a controlled setting, such as a laboratory, or with an experimental simulation. Usability testing allows testers to collect both qualitative and quantitative data as the end user performs a real task or set of tasks. Three ways to discover how a user approaches a Web site include the thinking-aloud protocol, the codiscovery method, and the question-asking protocol (Hom 1996).

> With the thinking-aloud protocol, one user is observed as he or she tackles a sample task. The user is asked to express aloud any options, feelings, or thoughts while testing the Web site.

> The codiscovery method is similar to the thinking-aloud protocol, but it requires the observation of two users working together to perform a task. This method is best used when the Web site is intended for use in a team environment.

> The question-asking protocol actively seeks feedback from the users by asking direct questions about the task being performed or the Web site.

Each of these processes can be performed during any phase of Web site usability testing.

THE GOAL OF USABILITY TESTING

As presented in this book, usability testing is not a tool of validation but one of evaluation. The goal of the test is simply to tell you whether your site is achieving the said goal, i.e., working. In essence, a "working" site is one that is literally usable. A site that is usable would encompass the four factors of Web site usability as identified by Rubin (1994). That is, the Web site should be not only useful but also effective and learnable, and one that generates high user satisfaction.

Usefulness establishes whether the Web site does what the user needs it to do.

Effectiveness refers to the ease of use to achieve the desired task.

Learnability relates to how easy it is to learn an application and to move from being a novice to being a skilled user.

User satisfaction relates to the user's attitude about the Web site—how enjoyable it is to use it.

The goal of the test is to uncover any problems or stumbling blocks that may interfere with navigation through a Web site. Usability testing determines the fit of the design to the intended users.

PROCESS OVERVIEW

In usability testing, end users complete a set of real tasks while test observers collect information on behavior, expectations, and other empirical data. The test renders explicit user feedback about the Web site design, revealing the strengths and weaknesses of the site. The results are then used to make changes and improvements affecting Web site effectiveness, usefulness, and user satisfaction.

Web site usability testing involves both qualitative and quantitative research. Qualitative research includes anecdotal feedback directly from customers, whereas the quantitative research includes data analysis. Greene, Caracelli, and Graham (1989) also add that a combination of these two methods of research adds both scope and breadth to the study.

Limitations

However, there are limitations to Web site usability testing. Two major limitations are related to factors of reliability and validity. According to Hernon (1994, p. 2), reliability is "the extent to which the same results are produced on repeated samples of the same population." Subsequently, there are two types of validity—internal and external. Internal validity is "the extent to which researchers measure what they intend to measure." External validity is "the generalizability or representativeness of [the] study findings."

Wheat and Greenberg (1998) identified several reliability and validity factors. The reliability factors that may limit Web site usability testing would include the following:

The testing of users who are not classified (such as atypical users) may increase the risk of gathering unreliable data.

Individual variation within the test population may make it less likely to ensure that the data collected is reliable.

The validity factors that can limit Web site usability testing would include the following:

The data collected in the usability test depends on the accuracy of the test tasks, scenarios of the search processes, and testing environment.

The results of the Web site testing are not generalizable to the entire user population.

Usability testing is beneficial to all aspects of the Web site development. It can help designers explore other design ideas; validate and refine design, systems, and mechanisms in the design and innovation stage; and help understand the user's acceptance of the design in the implementation and evaluation phase. Successful testing establishes or reinforces design standards.

WHY DO USABILITY TESTING?

Research by Rouffs (1991), Lansdale and Ormerod (1994), and Galitz (1997) affirms the fact that the computer interface affects usability. Therefore, it would seem likely that there is also an interrelationship between Web site design and usability—so much so that the overall success of a Web site transcends to an issue of that which is utilitarian (e.g., "good site" means easy to use). At best, usability testing can provide valuable insight into how utilitarian your library's Web site is.

Developments in information access technology are diminishing the traditional boundaries of libraries. The technological advances are enabling libraries to provide seamless access to library services. At best, the symbiosis of technology and librarianship catapults library and information science professionals to take a more proactive role in the Web design, development, and implementation processes. An additional (and often misplaced) role is that of addressing usability issues. Librarians and developers alike tend to concentrate more on information integrity and less on the impact of the actual presentation of the online or electronic information or service.

The strong precedent to employ usability testing is due to the growth of the Web. Unfortunately, the same expertise that serves as an advantage in Web development can be a disadvantage when it comes to Web site usability and subsequent Web site usability testing. Usability testing allows Web site developers to gain insights from the perspective of one who really knows if the site's design is helpful—the user. The incorporation of usability testing into the Web site development process increases the value of the Web site as well as affirms the said organization's integrity.

The Five Values of Usability Testing

Most librarians may need to rally buy-in. Enlisting buy-in from colleagues and supervisors can be a challenge, especially when this process is conceptualized as an optional component in the Web development process. (See chapter 3.) However, Web site usability testing should not be considered an option but a necessary facet of the Web site developmental stages.

To advocate buy-in, librarians may want to consider the following value points. These points, the five values of Web site usability testing, are concepts presented by Wheat and Greenberg (1998), who provide several arguments in support of usability testing.

1. *Understand the difference between usability testing and a research study.* The two methods differ in that usability testing identifies problem areas, whereas research verifies the existence of a theory.

2. *Incorporate real users.* Web site testing involves users who are representative of the targeted audience. By engaging real users, developers can understand the specific needs of users.

3. *Employ real tasks.* Web site testing involves tasks that are representative of how the Web site is or should be used. The incorporation of real tasks may provide a wealth of information on the areas that are in need of change or improvement.

4. *Observe and record meticulously.* The purpose of the test is to observe the participants' ability to perform the said tasks; therefore, record comments or questions about the Web site as well as users' behaviors. This observation and recording distinguishes usability testing from focus groups, surveys, or beta testing.

5. *Inattention to data implications is risky.* The qualitative and quantitative data collected from the participants (as well as the observer's notes) are analyzed and categorized, thus pinpointing the problem areas of the Web site. This process of categorizing and identifying enables you to prioritize problems as well as identify solutions.

At best, library professionals routinely see, promote, or equate themselves as the "agents" for the users; however, no one speaks better on behalf of the user than the user him or herself. Librarians and developers should always employ usability testing in every phase of their Web site development process as a way to bridge the traditional gap between the designer and user.

KEY PLAYERS

There are primarily two categories of key players—the usability testing team and the end users. According to Wheat and Greenberg (1998), the ideal Web site usability test team would include a designer, usability specialist, evaluation specialist, technical communicators, trainers, and marketing and customer assistance personnel. Identification of your library's Web site usability testing team should be parallel to Wheat and Greenberg's team suggestion. Although your library may not have all or some of the team members recommended, it is important to identify and enlist the librarians or library personnel who provide or can provide the said task. For example, the usability specialist would be responsible for facilitating the Web site usability testing process. The designer can provide the technical expertise regarding changes to the Web site. An evaluation specialist would be responsible for the analysis of the data. Technical communication and documentation would be the task of the technical communicators. The trainer could walk trainees through the various stages of the testing process. The marketing (or customer assistance) personnel would be responsible for the promotion and recruitment of the usability testing participants.

The integral role of end users in Web site usability testing cannot be overstated. The value of their input as well as their overall participation should be respected. It is imperative to communicate to the participants that their input is valuable and will make a difference. Participants in the Web site usability testing process should be assured of the confidentiality of their input. They should also be given the option of withdrawing from the testing at any time during the process.

Considering the involvement of key players in addition to equipment and time, the Web site usability testing process can become very expensive. More advanced Web site usability testing includes using outside testers or consultants, professional usability laboratories, and technological tracking devices. However, there is a less complicated and less expensive yet effective way to conduct usability tests of Web sites. This book provides the cost-effective guidelines on how librarians and any other persons involved in the Web development process can perform usability tests to assess the effectiveness and functionality of their Web sites and maintain the integrity required for any research and development process.

Let's begin!

REFERENCES

Galitz, W. O. 1997. *The Essential Guide to User Interface Design: An Introduction to GUI Design Principles and Techniques.* New York: John Wiley.

Greene, J. C., V. J. Caracelli, and W. F. Graham. 1989. "Toward a Conceptual Framework for Mixed-method Evaluation Designs." *Educational Evaluation and Policy Analysis* 11, no. 3: 255–74.

Hernon, P. 1994. *Statistics: A Component of the Research Process.* Norwood, N.J.: Ablex.

Hom, J. T. 1996. The Usability Methods Toolbox. Available: http://www.best.com/~jthom/usability/usahome.htm. Last update: June 1998. Accessed: Jan. 2000.

Kaplan, R. 2000. E-mail message to CM! Winters inquiry.

Lansdale, M. W., and T. Ormerod. 1994. *Understanding Interfaces: A Handbook of Human-Computer Dialogue.* Computers and People Series, edited by B. R. Gaines and A. Monk. San Diego, Calif.: Academic Press.

McGrath, J. E. 2000. "Methodology Matters: Doing Research in the Behavioral and Social Sciences." In *Readings in Human-Computer Interaction: Toward the Year 2000,* edited by R. M. Baecker and others. San Francisco, Calif.: Morgan Kaufmann.

Rouffs, J. A. J. 1991. *The Man-Machine Interface.* Vol. 15 of *Vision and Visual Dysfunction,* edited by John Cronly-Dillon. Boca Raton, Fla.: CRC Press.

Rubin, J. 1994. *Handbook of Usability Testing.* New York: Wiley.

Usernomics. 1999. Available: www.usernomics.com. Accessed: Feb. 2000.

Wheat, B., with S. Greenberg. 1998. Observational Usability Testing. Available: http://www.cpsc.ucalgary.ca/~saul/681/1998/observ_usab_testing/681contents.html. Accessed March 2000.

2

Web Design Guidelines

Researchers who address interface design often resort to empirical and contextual studies that discuss the various aspects of the user's Web design needs. Others may choose to rely on their own clairvoyant ideas about users' expertise when developing Web sites. Both novice and skilled Web site developers will consult the vast market of instructional Web development books, articles, and Web sites in an effort to develop that "good" Web site.

The information presented in these books, articles, and Web sites are more or less promotions of suggested guidelines, style guides, checklists, and tips. The purpose of this chapter is not to evaluate or recapitulate that volume of information. Perhaps you can consider this chapter a decoder of all that information you have ever heard about developing a Web site, ranging from the tedious efforts of cognitive processing to the widely circulated marketing jargon KISS (keep it simple, stupid). All this information falls into four basic principles:

keep the end user in mind

achieve superiority through simplicity

improve performance through design

refine and iterate

KEEP THE END USER IN MIND

The first and foremost rule in designing and developing a Web page is to *keep the end user in mind* at all times. Web designers and developers routinely come under fire for having someone other than the end user in mind, such as the boss or even themselves. Understanding the dynamics of the work environment, the fulfillment of a boss's desires is sometimes unavoidable. Others approach the Web design process as a great canvas of some sort that serves as an artistic platform on which to display their technological savvy. The Web development project is not an artistic covert exhibit. It is, however, an opportunity to demonstrate your ability to put the user first—then everything else follows logically.

You can identify the end user at the onset and throughout the development process by using a planning guide as well as developing a user profile. The five key questions a planning guide should ask are

What is the purpose of the site?

Who are the users?

What are the users' capabilities?

What is the intended use of the Web site compared with the user's wants?

Where will the site be hosted, and what are the capabilities of the host?

The user profile need not be filled with excruciating details about *each* user, but it should contain some generalizations about the intended audience. To begin, perhaps you could enlist a few default assumptions.

Know your end user. All parties involved in the design process should have some sense of the targeted population through demographics such as population count, position, ethnicity, gender, etc. The site should be representative of its intended audience. This representation can be achieved in every aspect of the page, including content. For example, some Web sites may attempt to make their sites more personal by adding photos or cartoons of people. Other Web sites may use examples to demonstrate the use of the site or relative content. The images of people and the subjects of the examples should include a balanced distribution of a diverse population. This diverse representation is not limited to ethnicity but includes those with varying educational abilities, physical capabilities, and cultural dynamics.

All systems are not created equal. The user profile should by default assume that some people have limited system capabilities for remote access. The users accessing the site will undoubtedly have a wide variety of platform, browser, and connection capabilities. It may even be best to develop the site as if the intended audience would be using a relatively low-end (i.e., older, slower) computer.

Be mindful of end users with physical limitations. The third default assumption is that your Web site must accommodate persons with various physical capabilities. Therefore, the site should adhere to the accessibility requirements prescribed by your institution or other agencies. After all, a site should be accessible to all end users regardless of their abilities.

Perhaps the best way to keep the user in mind is to know who your intended audience is or what type of user you are trying to attract to your Web site. Begin by asking not only what type of persons would use this site but also why they would refer to your Web site.

ACHIEVE SUPERIORITY THROUGH SIMPLICITY

"KISS" is perhaps the most widely circulated Web design caveat. This principle serves as the technological proverb often quoted when discussing a design that attempts to manage or resist development complexity. In an effort to avoid the familiar term "keep it simple, stupid" the KISS acronym could be translated as "keep it superior and simple" or "keep it superior through simplicity."

The information needs of the end user are constantly subjected to change; therefore, the information needs are multifarious and dynamic. Superior Web designs satisfy those needs by keeping all aspects of the Web site, whether it is content or presentation, simple. And simple can be hard—but once simplicity is achieved, it is superior.

Organization and Format

A library Web site will provide mostly documents, graphics, and data. The Web designers and developers initially determine what items are made available through links and electronic files. The materials should be organized in a way that is familiar to the end user, such as alphabetically, chronologically, geographically, or topically.

A superior site will also promote simplicity by developing a consistent look and feel throughout the site. Site consistency means that there is a system or structured format for presenting the information so that it is logically understood by even a less-than-savvy Internet user. A site that is consistent encourages user familiarity. It is the concept of familiarity that helps users interpret your site as being simple and easy to use and makes them likely to return to and promote it to other users.

Fonts and Color

The Web site attributes considered sensitive to consistency are choice of font and color. Consider the representation of consistency in font; this is called *typology*. Typology is the use of a font style (i.e., **bold,** *italic,* underline, etc.) and type (i.e., New Times Roman, Arial, Book Antiqua). Be wary of using more than two or three different fonts because more than three will make your site appear complicated. Use some of the more basic fonts like New Times Roman and Arial that are more likely to be compatible from system to system.

Designers will also use color to help the user gain familiarity or a "feel" of the Web site. Use of the same colors in certain places, such as making all exit buttons blue, encourages consistency. Furthermore, consider the psychological aspects of color that evoke certain feelings. For example, large quantities of red can make people feel angry or agitated.

Language

Perhaps the most unavoidable concept that makes for Web site superiority through simplicity is the function of language. Language not only communicates content but also provides the tone of the information being presented. A simple Web site incorporates language that can be understood by both the most advanced and the novice user. For example, the University of Illinois at Chicago main library's reference resources Web site incorporates the use of clear and concise instruction into its Web design. It provides a page that is simple enough to aid a novice user yet it does not appear mundane to the more advanced user. (See figure 2.1.)

IMPROVE PERFORMANCE THROUGH DESIGN

A Web site is not the same as a book; therefore, the design and development of a Web page should not be approached as such. *In actuality, a Web site is a service.* It is different from a book because there is no guaranteed static presentation. When using a book, the reader cannot change things such as the font or color. In contrast, the user, not the author, ultimately controls the Web page; end users can change things such as the font and color of the page. In addition, your library's Web site may look different depending on the browser and monitor being used. It is possible, however, to embed some sense of Web

FIGURE 2.1
University of Illinois at Chicago Library's Reference Web Page

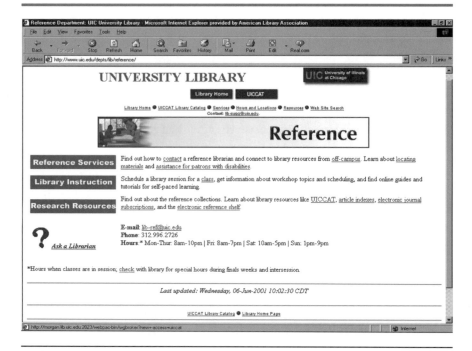

Used with permission of the University of Illinois at Chicago Library.

site control through the design, ultimately enhancing the site's performance. The three points to remember about this principle of performance through design are speed, appearance, and usability.

Speed

Do your users wait for a site to download? More often than not, they won't unless they are using a pretty fast system. Do not assume that everyone using remote access has a fast computer system. One sure way to frustrate your user is to provide a page that is full of graphics and large files that take a long time to download. Therefore, limit the number of graphics, and resist using large files that can decelerate the downloading of a Web page.

Other ways to increase the download speed of your Web site include separating large pages into smaller pages. Using thumbnails for larger graphics gives the user a sense of control of time by deciding whether they want to wait for the download. Furthermore, designers may want to consider reusing graphic images because they will already be cached.

Appearance

Appearance is important because it has an immediate impact on a user's opinion about your Web site. Keep in mind when designing that although the Web page can be long, only a small part appears in the browser window. Therefore, place the most important items on the first screen (i.e., list of online databases, hours of operation, and phone numbers), and if at all possible, limit the pages to four screens. In most cases, you will want to design pages that can be viewed fully on the smallest screens (e.g., 15 inches).

As stated earlier, consistency in font and color is appealing to the user. The consistency enhances the user's familiarity with the site, and users can learn for themselves how to navigate the Web site. Suggested elements for consistency are not limited to color or font but also include logs, location of navigation links, layout, and site identification.

Usability

Usability is important because this is one of the integral ways a user determines whether to return to your site. Provide the user with easily identified navigation aids, with at least one always being the link back to the home page or start of the section. It is not enough to simply say "click here." Likewise, information on the page should be presented in a logical format. However, remember that what is logical to you may not necessarily be logical to others (hence the value of usability testing).

In most instances, instituting performance through design can create a real challenge. On one hand, designers must deal with the question of how to present information in a way that is not restrictive (or excessive). On the other hand, they must take into consideration the impediment of speed through downloads (i.e., pictures and images) when designing an attractive site while maintaining a more-than-acceptable level of usability. At this point, simplicity must give way to functionality. Consider once again the University of Illinois' Main Library's Web page that provides information about the vast resources available to its library users. The library's resources Web page (figure 2.2) maintains performance through design by relying on few images and concise descriptions with links.

FIGURE 2.2
University of Illinois at Chicago Library's Resources Web Page

Screen A

Screen B

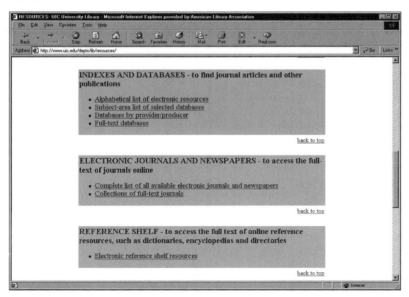

Screen C

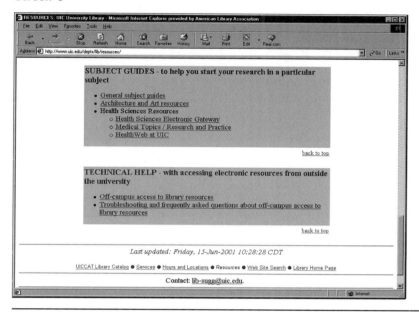

Used with permission of the University of Illinois at Chicago Library.

REFINE AND ITERATE

Refine means "to purge"; *iterate* simply means "to do repeatedly." The principle of refine and iterate implies that the site should be examined on a regular basis. The ordeal of designing and developing the Web site will seem easy compared with the upkeep of your Web site. Web designers should refine and iterate the site on a regular basis as a function in the development process. This should be done every four to six months to take into account dynamics such as new technology, updated information, or broken links.

The designer must ensure that the content of a Web site is current, ultimately removing or replacing out-of-date information. Those responsible for carrying out this task should examine all the links to make sure that they still work.

Instituting a feedback function in the Web design can serve as a useful aid. The users serve as the lookout persons, reporting any problems or concerns that may have been overlooked. The Web designers should investigate reported concerns and make subsequent revisions to that site.

3

Getting Buy-in

For your Web site usability testing to function optimally you will want to share with others its importance, value, and practicality. It is in sharing this information and, in some instances, providing education about Web site usability testing that you can demonstrate that this is not just a good idea but a necessary and achievable idea. At best, we are talking about getting buy-in.

The word *buy-in* is often seen as one of those cosmopolitan change-management terms. Sometimes the term generates cynicism by those who may have had their fill of change-management techniques. The misconception of buy-in is often the result of misunderstanding, thereby contributing to subsequent misuse. So, let's begin this discussion with the basics as a way to establish and, in some instances, restore credibility to this process.

WHAT IS BUY-IN?

Fundamentally, buy-in is a communication tool used to institute change. It entails gathering support from people whose partnership you need to achieve the desired change. The people whose partnership is deemed necessary to accomplish conversion are also known as "stakeholders" or the "audience." You, on the other hand, who would introduce the idea of change would be known as the "solicitor" or the "advocate." And as the advocate, or solicitor, you undertake the proactive effort to raise awareness about the importance and value of Web site usability testing.

In understanding buy-in, it is important to know that there are two types of buy-in—passive and active. Passive buy-in means that people go with the proposed idea because they "have to," unlike active buy-in in which people go with the proposed idea because they want to. In essence, it is the effect of commitment leveraged by attitude; the appropriate balance between these two types of buy-in can make all the difference in any project effort.

To understand the dynamic of passive and active buy-in, consider the relationship of authority between the person soliciting buy-in and the identified partners. A person with authority advocating buy-in can instigate passive buy-in by essentially stating, "It *will* be done." Alternatively, a person with less authority could do the same by insisting, "It *should* be done." Either way, the solicitation of support will more than likely lead to opposition, and that can take away from the success of any project initiative, even leading to the point of project demise. On the other hand, those same people, regardless of authority, can advocate active buy-in by stressing, "It *can* be done." By incorporating this approach, discontented and unwilling partners are more apt to embrace your idea and become champions of the desired change.

It is also important to note that buy-in does not mean authorization, nor does it ensure project viability. Getting buy-in affords you the opportunity to let others "hear you out," understand your initiative, and then willingly commit to the idea. The viability of your project is best assessed through a good proposal. The objective of the proposal, whether presented formally or informally, is to provide a comprehensive evaluation of the significant issue for the purpose of making a decision. The objective of getting buy-in is to rally the necessary partners who agree that your idea makes sense and is worth achieving.

THE ESSENTIALS OF GETTING BUY-IN

Getting buy-in does not have less value than the proposal process. Buy-in is important: it can help you gain acceptance of the idea and, more importantly, develop a cohesive group of advocates. Getting buy-in not only requires leadership, education, and teamwork but also an understanding of some of the essential elements to the buy-in process. The identified essential elements include developing subject-matter expertise; proving usability testing works; making the buy-in process personal; being straightforward; and anticipating backlash and welcoming feedback.

Become the Subject-Matter Expert

Getting buy-in at the onset requires that you know—truly know—Web site usability testing. Therefore, you must become the subject-matter expert. The subject in this instance is Web site usability testing and the Web site itself. Becoming the subject-matter expert means that you are on the alert for all information pertaining to Web site usability testing. In becoming the expert, you don't necessarily have to know everything, but you should know enough to appear confident to colleagues.

One way to assess your subject-matter expertise is testing your ability to respond to inquiries. You can assess your knowledge by generating your own question-and-answer list that includes who, what, when, why, and how. For example, ask yourself:

Who are the stakeholders?

Who can do Web site usability testing?

What is a Web site?

What is Web site usability testing?

What are the effects of the process?

When is it a good time (and not a good time) to apply Web site usability testing?

How does Web site usability testing work?

How does the successful (and unsuccessful) application of Web site usability testing affect Web development?

Prove Web Site Usability Testing Works

The proposal and subsequent implementation of any idea means change, and change in most environments can be considered an annoyance. One way to combat this annoyance is to be prepared to provide proof that Web site usability testing works. This means understanding and ultimately communicating the value of Web site usability testing.

There are several ways to prove value. One way to prove value is to explain how Web site usability testing can help achieve library goals. Back this up with journal articles containing both qualitative and quantitative data regarding the successful implementation of Web site usability testing in other settings. Another way to prove it can work is by explaining the costs (financial and nonfinancial) of not successfully implementing Web site usability testing. One of the most powerful ways to prove it works is to share the experiences of other libraries that have employed Web site usability testing.

Personalize the Issue

Converting Web site usability testing into a personal issue really means answering "What is in it for me?" In doing so, you could realize what are or could be the stakeholders' apprehensions so you can prepare to address them by providing the necessary information to ease any uncertainty. Examples of questions asked by administrative-level personnel could include the following:

How does this benefit the library?

Why should we do this?

What will it cost?

Will it be worth the investment?

What type of commitment is needed?

Similarly, library personnel may ask:

How will this affect my job performance?

Will I need to learn any new skills? If so, what new training will I need?

Be Straightforward

Don't try to impress the stakeholders with fancy terms or jargon. Use language that is not only suitable for your audience but that is comfortable for you as well. Furthermore, provide the whole truth about the Web site usability testing process, advising your colleagues of the challenges and the accomplishments. After all, no process is flawless. Remember you are trying to gain the respect and trust necessary for active buy-in. Anticipate backlash, and welcome feedback.

In any process that requires change and, ultimately, proof that it works, be prepared for backlash. Backlash should not be seen as some uprising against your desired change. At best, it is a signal that people are receiving the information and thinking about it. Plus, without some backlash you could be headed toward a passive buy-in. Sure ways to effectively manage backlash are to respond to any inquiries or comments, being confident in your level of subject-matter expertise, ability to prove it works, tact in personalizing the issue, and straightforwardness.

Feedback is also imperative to the buy-in process. It affords you the opportunity to familiarize yourself with the concerns and expectations of the required partners. Furthermore, it can be a resource of additional ideas that can make the Web site usability testing project even more successful.

MANAGING THE BUY-IN PROCESS

Getting buy-in, even under the most ideal circumstances, can be difficult. It is difficult because you are dealing with humans and not necessarily the technology. Your ability to effectively manage the buy-in process should be practical in every sense of the word. In doing so, you should take into consideration the dynamics of the library culture (i.e., academic, public, special, small, large, etc.).

Think of managing your buy-in process as an opportunity for creativity and initiative. You are creating opportunities to bring stakeholders together to communicate as well as to collaborate. Remember that these groups also have missions; therefore, it is important to connect the usability testing with these same priorities. It is also very important to devise an effective way to manage your buy-in process, which includes having a plan, establishing multilevel support and commitment, providing information seminars, and even exploring library policies and procedures manuals.

Prepare a Written Plan

Your plan to get buy-in should be thoughtful, clear, and concise. In essence, this is your strategy. When you prepare your plan to gain buy-in, you should be sure to include the necessary components—mission statement, goals, and objectives—that ultimately tie into the desired change. In your plan, be prepared to address issues about resources, barriers, and expectations. You must also identify and address any costs (financial and nonfinancial).

Your plan should also include a time line that identifies key activities and possible assignments of responsibilities of stakeholders. Furthermore, your written plan should address these four questions: Is it credible? Is it relevant? Is it worth it? And what action should be taken?

Establish Multilevel Support

Depending on your library culture, you will more than likely address a combination of stakeholders. An example of stakeholders includes administrators, business leaders, community leaders, campus community leaders, corporate officials, donors, education officials, elected officials, library users, library staff, special committees, task groups, professionals in related fields, researchers, students, and volunteers. You must identify which of these stakeholders are the necessary partners to bring Web site usability testing into fruition. It is also important to know why you need these partners and assess or rank the value of attaining their buy-in. In identifying stakeholders, target those persons who already work in some capacity with Web development. Remember—without the support from your library's leadership, a project may be likely to fail.

Bringing the selected groups together requires a commitment to reach out and to continue to make connections with these groups. It will not be easy at first, but persistence may very well get you the results you and your library are looking for to get this project off the ground.

Provide an Information Workshop

Once you have introduced the concept of usability testing and gotten the stakeholders' initial buy-in (i.e., attention), volunteer to organize an opportunity for these people to get together to further explore the idea. You might meet over lunch or set up an office bulletin board or discussion group Web page to share information and answer any questions or respond to any concerns.

Propose Amended Policies and Procedures

More than likely, your library has a policy or procedure manual on Web development. It is important to review those items and familiarize yourself with them. You may find that your proposal to introduce or integrate Web site usability testing may require adjustments to those policies and procedures. For example, your particular library might have a policy that limits graphics on the library interface because they interfere with the integrity of the Web site. However, after a few rounds of testing, the library Web team finds that students respond more positively to a combination of text and graphics. In that case, the library Web team will have to see if the policy on graphics and other visual literacy methodologies could be reexamined or revised.

4

Preassessment and Planning

You have demonstrated your expertise on the topic, and you have gotten buy-in from the targeted stakeholders. Now what? Now you are ready to rally the troops and get started with the testing. In these next chapters, you will learn more about the actual process of Web site usability testing. Of particular value is the importance of preassessment and planning that can help you narrow your usability testing focus and know what areas to concentrate on.

PREASSESSMENT

For most library Web sites, a variety of areas could be looked at closely through usability testing, including the online catalog, electronic resources, remote access capability, library hours, staff information, etc. Which areas should you initially focus on for the usability test? Unless your library has been receiving numerous complaints about how difficult it is to find a book using the library Web site, it is very hard to detect when and where people are having problems. Unfortunately, many customers will abandon the library Web site in frustration instead of seeking help from library staff members. Therefore, even though the library staff members may think that customers are having the most difficulty locating books, in reality the areas of confusion may be figuring out how to use the online interlibrary loan form or how to access electronic journals remotely or a combination of both. To narrow down the areas to concentrate on, obtain some baseline or initial data through preassessment. The goal of the preassessment plan is to develop a keen understanding of the Web site users and their goals when interacting with the Web site.

The most common assessment tools used are print surveys, online surveys, and focus groups. Depending on the culture of your library, time commitments, and financial restraints, you can use all or just one of these preassessment tools. Keep in mind that this should not be complicated. Instead, it should be a quick way to narrow down the areas to focus on for the actual usability test.

Print and Online Surveys

A survey is the fastest way to obtain information. A print survey can be placed at the reference area, by the computers, by the information desk, in the rest rooms, or by the front door. An online survey, if you have someone with the technical expertise to create it and monitor the results, is even better because people can access it outside the library. An online survey is especially helpful if the library has remote users who do not frequent the library. In either case, if you decide to develop a survey, keep the questions simple. Ask if the person has found what he or she was looking for, and if not, where the problem occurred. (See figure 4.1.)

Decide how many surveys to distribute to customers and how many completed surveys will be enough to look for patterns. You probably do not have to survey 500 people to find out that some people simply cannot find out if the library is open on the weekend. To start with, collect a small subset of your customers—you can always collect more surveys later.

If you use a survey, remember the following points:

Often customers will say "everything is great." That may be true at that moment, but they may have forgotten the time they spent four hours searching the library Web site in vain. Nevertheless, retain these people as potential usability test participants at a later date.

Make sure to include important demographic information on the survey. Verifiable data is needed to aid in the selection of usability test participants, such as gender, age, and education.

Many customer comments may not focus on the questions asked. For example, some comments might focus on library environment issues such as the comfort of the chairs instead of targeted concerns about the Web site.

FIGURE 4.1
Sample Survey

Directions: Please answer the following questions to help us identify our user/ customer groups and to better serve you.

Name (optional) _____

Phone or e-mail address (optional) _____

1. How often do you access the library Web site? (Circle one.)

   Once a month   3–5 times a month

   2–3 times a month   6+ times a month

2. Did you find what you were looking for? _____ yes _____ no

3. Please describe your experience using the library Web site. (Circle one.)

   easy   confusing

   difficult   other _____

4. Have you had problems finding information on the Web site? ___ yes ___ no

   If yes, please tell us what areas, if any, confuse or frustrate you?

   _____

   _____

5. Would you use/visit the library Web site again? _____ yes _____ no

6. In the next few weeks, we are going to take a closer look at our Web site. Would you be interested in helping us out for $5? _____ yes _____ no

   If so, please remember to include your phone number and/or e-mail address.

Thank you.

Even though they have limitations, surveys can be a great tool if you have limited resources and limited time. An overall positive outcome from conducting a survey before the usability test is that the people who participate can become potential participants for the usability test.

Focus Groups

If you have the time or funding, you might want to try using focus groups for preassessment. This option will not work for libraries whose main focus or customers use distance learning or who live in other locations. (In this case, the best preassessment tool is to use an online survey.) Focus groups are a tremendous tool because they allow you to ask follow-up questions and obtain additional information, which is hard to do with surveys. Focus groups frequently help many people remember an incident that they may not have recalled if they were completing a survey.

If your organization wants to test its external Web site designed for the general population, consider outsourcing the recruiting of focus group participants. A focus group service may cost between $1,000 and $1,500 for 5 participants.

If your library does not have the funds for outside services, you can recruit participants for a focus group session by placing advertisements in the library, by the computer terminals, and on the library Web site. Use an ad on the library Web site if the library customers are people who are in town but who don't come into the library that often. Some kind of incentive is essential because many people will not come into the library for an hour without knowing how it will benefit them.

The ideal size for a focus group is usually between five and ten participants. You can entice people to participate by

defining participation as community service

offering a cash payment or gift certificates, T-shirts, copy cards, food, etc.

providing public recognition for groups of people who attend the focus group sessions (for example, the Friends of the library or the senior citizens association could be recognized in the library newsletter or on the bulletin board)

having a contest or competition between units for the most participants recruited

Choose a centralized location that is comfortable and free from distractions such as noise, traffic, or telephones. The session length can vary, but it should be an hour or less, especially if participants are not being paid. Two people are usually needed to administer the focus group session: a moderator, who will ask the questions and facilitate the dialogue, and a recorder. The moderator must be someone who can remain unbiased throughout the focus group session and who knows when to follow up with additional questions to clarify responses. The recorder writes down all the participants' comments and transcribes them later or gets permission from the participants to use a tape recorder. At the end of these sessions, participants can be asked if they'd like to participate in the actual usability testing at a later date.

Continue with additional sessions and new participants until you start to see patterns emerge. This usually means scheduling four to five focus group sessions. You may need to continue with additional sessions. If you have the time to conduct more focus group sessions, it can definitely be worthwhile.

FIGURE 4.2
Sample Questions for Focus Groups

1. How often do you access the library Web site?

2. When you access the library Web site, what are you usually looking for?

3. How often are you successful in obtaining what you want?

4. Which areas of the library Web site are the easiest to use?

5. Which areas are the hardest or most confusing for you?

6. Would you be interested in helping us improve the library Web site for $5? If so, please supply your phone number and/or e-mail address.

7. Name two things that you like about our overall library Web site and two things that need improvement.

However, remember that the main objective is to look for initial patterns or areas to concentrate on to develop in depth during the usability testing.

The focus group sessions should gather the following information:

demographics of participant (name, gender, occupation, and contact information)

general impressions of the Web site (likes, dislikes, comparisons or contrasts with other sites, etc.)

new ideas and creative concepts for the Web site

diagnosis of potential problems (for example, terminology, icons, placement of instructions, etc.)

See figure 4.2 for sample focus group questions.

THE USABILITY TESTING TEAM

You will want to decide who will be on the usability testing team in advance of the actual testing so they can be a part of the preassessment process. This will greatly influence how well the usability tests are conducted and the data is analyzed, thereby increasing the value of the testing results. The team should be composed of a variety of personnel who are engaged in designing and maintaining the Web site. For example, personnel who are responsible for content, design, technical support, customer support, etc., should serve as members of the team. An ideal number of team members is between four and seven, although one librarian can conduct usability testing on his or her own (see the next section). However, if your library has the following positions, a possible configuration might include

- the Web master, a systems person, or anyone who makes frequent changes or updates to the library Web site
- a technical services person (cataloger or acquisitions person) who is usually responsible for cataloging and acquiring print, electronic, and digital resources
- a public services or reference librarian who is usually in contact with the customers on a daily basis through reference work, outreach, or instruction
- one or two new librarians or staff members who can provide a pair of fresh eyes and an unbiased view of the library Web site
- the library administrator, manager, or supervisor who can help with getting buy-in if the Web team requires approval for making major changes to the Web site after usability testing

Although the Web team is explained in greater detail in chapter 5, do not take this important step lightly. The Web team should be willing to actively participate throughout the entire process, although only two team members are present during the actual testing. The rest of the team helps create the test, analyze results, and revise the Web site. The library administrator needs to be part of the actual usability test. Once the library administrator or manager sees a participant getting frustrated or not finding something on the library Web site, it is easier to persuade the administrator to allow the Web team to make the necessary changes.

There are a variety of approaches to familiarizing and training the test team on usability testing techniques. Simply reading the literature is not a holistic approach, particularly if team members are not all librarians who actually use and instruct others in the use of the interface being tested. Search your local area for any institution, organization, or company that may have conducted usability tests. Ask if a usability team representative would be willing to come to your group and speak about that experience, or interview that person and report back to the group. This is a practical approach to becoming familiar with the ins and outs of the real testing environment versus the "just-the-facts" theory as presented in some of the literature. A review of some of the "how we did it" literature will also assist in grounding the team members in the theoretical and practical issues involved in actual testing situations.

Teams for Solo Librarians

If you are in a corporate or school library and are a solo librarian or have a very small staff, how do you create a Web usability testing team? At first this may appear to be an insurmountable hurdle, but this challenge provides a great opportunity to get others in your organization involved in the decision-making process. In fact, the only difference between Web usability testing in a larger library and in one with a solo librarian is the level of flexibility. For example, you might solicit Web team members who are part of the administration, teachers, corporate employees, or customers. Having people on your Web team who are your customers will also help with positive public relations because as things change for the better on your Web interface, members of the Web team will talk about this to your other customers.

To recruit outside members on your Web team, first you will want to involve any library staff members who are working for you within the organization. If not, still follow the guidelines from the previous section on Web teams. Contact the Web master and see if he or she can be a part of the Web team. If you do not have a Web master, ask anyone who enjoys working with computers and has previous Web experience. Also remember to send out e-mails or mailings to members of your organization asking for volunteers. Plan to have the different duties within the Web team well thought out in advance so the person can respond to specific duties. Make sure that the ad, memo, or e-mail stresses the flexibility for the people involved. Another selling point for potential usability team members to participate is that the project looks good on a résumé. Highlighting the technology, Web design, and maintenance aspects of the project and the potential for learning and growth could attract ambitious people who are willing to help out.

Your team members' time will be limited, and they might not be able to follow the project all the way through from start to finish. Therefore, you will have to multitask the majority of the work and have the Web team members multitask specific duties to keep the project moving along smoothly. Additional information and detailed steps for solo librarians are explained in chapters 5 and 6.

5

Preparing and Evaluating the Usability Test

This chapter will go over some of the important steps of the usability test process after selecting the Web team. The steps will also include examples and possible ideas that you can print out and use or adapt to your particular library. This chapter will not go over the actual test, as it is provided in detail in chapter 6.

ESTABLISH GOALS AND OBJECTIVES

Before the Web usability team starts generating different tasks for the participants, they need to set goals and objectives. What is the final outcome of the usability testing project? Do you want to change one area of the library interface or all the areas? If you decided to do some preassessment research, the Web team will already know of some areas of confusion. For example, if the Web usability testing team decides to conduct focus groups on several target audiences and many of them stated that the electronic resources section is confusing, this should become an automatic goal. Doing the preliminary research using surveys, focus groups, or other methods will help eliminate any confusion on where to get started when developing goals and objectives. If the Web team decided not to use preliminary data, they can just decide to make individual sections within their Web interface their individual goals and objectives. For example, separate goals with objectives can be created for the online catalog page, electronic journals, branch library information, Web resources, etc. One of your goals and objectives might look like the following:

Goal: Using usability testing and making changes on our Web interface, participants will find our online catalog page more user friendly.

Objective: After conducting usability testing and making changes, 80 percent of the participants tested will be able to find a book and an article on our online catalog page.

Note that your library Web team could decide that 5 out of 10, or 50 percent, is the acceptable number. It all depends on the expectations of the particular library.

DEVELOP THE TASKS OR QUESTIONS

For each round of usability testing, the Web team has to develop a set of tasks or questions that directly reflect specific goals and objectives. These tasks should require the participant to find something on the library Web site. Make sure the team keeps the tasks to a minimum because too many can frustrate or tire participants. This definitely happens when the Web team asks for the same reworded task over and over. To check for redundancy, sometimes it's good to write down what kind of information the Web team wants to obtain from each task. The examples in figure 5.1 demonstrate how to include the rationale for each task. Although this rationale is not shown to participants, it helps the Web team remain focused so they do not give in to the temptation to include too many tasks. A good rule of thumb is probably seven to ten tasks maximum for a one-hour session.

The assumption from the tasks and questions in figure 5.1 is that the participants know how to find books (two tasks) but will have more problems finding articles and journal titles. Therefore, every team member needs to be part of the initial process of developing tasks and questions. Public service librarians will have knowledge about what areas baffle students; the technical support members, including catalogers and systems people, will help public service people understand why information is organized in a certain manner. All of these pieces of information will feed into the assumptions the team will make before developing the tasks or knowing which ones to emphasize more than others.

FIGURE 5.1
Sample Academic Library Web Site Usability Test

Objective: When given various tasks, 80 percent of the participants will successfully be able to complete each task to locate books, articles, and journals while searching the library Web site

Tasks and Questions

1. Find two books on capital punishment. (books)
2. Find out if the journal *Educational Policy* is in the library. (journal titles)
3. Find articles on business management. (articles)
4. Find an article and a book on animal testing. (article and book)
5. If the above article is not full text, see if it is in the library. (journal title)
6. What two things helped you the most when using the Web site?
7. What two things need improvement to help you more easily search the Web site?

The tasks in figure 5.2 also start with the easiest and slowly increase in difficulty. The main objective during the test is to keep the participant as comfortable and confident as possible. If a participant feels that he or she cannot complete the first task, the participant will become exceedingly more frustrated as the test continues.

The final two questions are very important. Most of the time the participants will be offering continuous feedback and suggestions while they are talking out loud. However, in some cases, the most valuable information will come from the participant final assessment because they might not voice out loud some important suggestions until the end. Questions 6 and 7 usually take only a few minutes to answer, but they are highly recommended as the final items. The tasks and questions in figure 5.1 will probably take thirty minutes to an hour to complete.

Figure 5.2 is an example from a public library environment.

The assumption in figure 5.2 is that the branch items are easier and that navigating through the online catalog is creating some problems; therefore, various online catalog tasks call for multiple search strategies, including an author search. Answering item 5 requires multiple steps to narrow down the online search to just videos. For item 6 the participant must use multiple steps to get the call number and branch information. All of the tasks or questions should be able to be completed within the targeted goal of thirty minutes to an hour.

Figure 5.3 is an example of a usability test from a school library environment. Notice that the objective states "teachers" instead of participants. If the

FIGURE 5.2
Sample Public Library Web Site Usability Test

Objective: When given various tasks, 70 percent of the participants will successfully be able to complete each task to locate books, videos, branch locations, and operating hours while searching the library Web site.

Tasks and Questions

1. Find a book on home gardening. (books using title or key word search)
2. Find when the Dupont (western) branch closes on Wednesday. (branch hours)
3. Do we have a branch named Manchaca? (branch)
4. Find books by Maya Angelou. (books using author search)
5. Does the library have any Jane Fonda videos? (videos)
6. Find which library has the video "Get in Shape NOW" by Donna Richardson. (video and branch)
7. What two things helped you the most when using the Web site?
8. What two things need improvement to help you more easily search the Web site?

FIGURE 5.3
Sample School Library Web Site Usability Test

Objective: When given various tasks, 70 percent of the teachers will successfully be able to complete each task to find Web resources and specialized resources when searching the library Web site.

Tasks and Questions

1. Find the "Best School Reference Sites for Science Classes" on the Web page. (Web resources)
2. Where does the library have information on creating online research modules? (Web resources)
3. Find the "Join an Educational Discussion Group" on the Web site. Locate the discussion group that provides information about educationally relevant Internet resources. (Web resources)
4. The library has a link to help you reserve books or articles for term papers and assignments. Find this link, and go through the process of reserving a book. (specialized resources)
5. [directed to specific teachers] Find which Web resource packages were created for your classroom instruction. (Web resources)
6. What two things helped you the most when using the Web site?
7. What two things need improvement to help you more easily search the Web site?

Web team knows it is going to conduct several rounds of testing, it can adapt the wording for targeted groups. This round of usability testing is an example of how usability testing can also educate participants. Notice all the questions or tasks are introducing the teacher to Web resources that may not be so well known. For example, if the teacher successfully completes item 3, he or she will know where appropriate discussion groups are located for his or her subject area. If the teacher does not successfully complete the task, the moderator can show the participant where the link is located. Then the moderator can solicit suggestions on where to better place the link within the library Web site. (See the sections on moderators and recorders later in this chapter.) By the end of the testing, the participant will have a better understanding of how school librarians can help teachers develop information literacy and what Web resources are available.

To summarize, when developing tasks or questions you should

make sure you develop goals and objectives first

know the rationale behind each item to eliminate redundancy

start with simple tasks or questions and slowly get more complex

if possible, use the usability test to educate the participants about your library Web site

keep the number of questions under ten so they can be completed in an hour, or you run the risk of losing the participant's interest

include summary questions such as "What did you like/not like?" to bring the process to a close

WRITE THE SCRIPT

A script will give the Web team and the participants a general guideline of what's going to happen. It should be short and concise (no more than two pages) and include some basic elements, which will be discussed in the following examples. The generic script should also be adaptable and easily modified from one test to another (especially if the Web team envisions multiple usability testing throughout a space of months). It should be read or followed verbatim if possible. Following are some common elements that should be included in an average script.

Purpose of the Test

When the Web team recruits participants, it's a good idea to follow the motto "Less is more." Sometimes with too much in-depth information the participants might become worried that they will not have the right computer skills or knowledge to complete the test. However, it is crucial to come up with an agreed-upon purpose of the test to communicate to the participants, especially during the day of the test. Most of the time the purpose of the test will be something like

> The library needs feedback from our clients, customers, patrons, etc., on our library Web site to make it more user friendly and easier to find research information.

Structure of the Test

Although the Web team might have briefly touched upon this point while recruiting participants, it is important to explain what's going to happen before starting the usability test. Sometimes, especially if a participant is nervous about being tested or analyzed, he or she will forget everything that was initially explained about the test. Some elements to include under this section of the script are

How long will the test take?

How many questions will you ask during the complete process?

Will participants have to complete demographic information or a presurvey?

Will participants have to think out loud?

If a recorder or another person is in the room, why are they there?

What kind of questions will the moderator ask?

What questions will the moderator answer or not answer?

Design of the Web Site

The Web team might have to explain to the participant about any inner pages that are not completed or links that are not active. This happens sometimes when the Web team is in the middle of making major changes and when the Web site is still in the "under construction" phase. Explain that the concept is there, but the team does not want to invest unnecessary time and energy inserting links or completing all the inner pages. At this point, it is important to let the participant know, before the test, that the Web site is a work in progress.

Disclaimer about the Testing

A disclaimer is one of the most important elements of the script. Especially if the participants are asked to think out loud, it is natural for them to feel inferior if they are not answering the questions correctly. This really occurs when the participant completely gives up on a task or question because he or she does not know the answer. Although as the tester, you might wonder why someone couldn't find such a simple answer, it is crucial to set a disclaimer about the test:

> The Web site and the design are what's being tested, not the person.

If the participant cannot find the answer to the question or gets frustrated, this statement should be restated:

> Thanks for pointing out this obvious error on our part. Tell us how this could be plainer or simpler or what makes more sense.

Disclaimers can be stated in many different ways, but overall the moderator wants the person to be as relaxed as possible during this very awkward process. The script shown in figure 6.3 is somewhat generic and can be adapted for your specific use.

The sample script separates what to say before and after you get into the test room. This will help put the person at ease and divide up the dialog so the moderator will not overwhelm the participant. The script is only one page long so it can easily be printed out and read directly word-for-word.

RECRUIT PARTICIPANTS FOR THE USABILITY TEST

This section is for people who need to get participants. However, if the Web team initially used preassessment, it's a good idea to retest some of those who previously participated.

One of the most frustrating points about the process is getting reliable participants. Libraries cannot test every person who accesses the library interface in the library or remotely. Moreover, even after attracting a list of potential participants, some people will not show up for their scheduled appointments. Therefore, it is crucial to develop a list of potential participants and a list of those who can serve as backups. This whole process can be made easier with a good plan and strategy, as outlined in the following sections.

Establishing a Target Market or Group

A target market or group is a group of people who are typical of your primary customers. It is created to make sure you have an adequate sample of all constituents you would like to test so results will be representative of that entire population while still being small enough to be manageable. It is mainly beneficial in qualitative research because this type of research is usually more anecdotal instead of scientific.

For example, if you work at an academic library, do you want more freshmen than graduate students? Are you just looking for incoming students rather than seasoned doctoral students? If you work at a public library, would you want someone from the library board to participate? How many elderly? How many young adults? A special library might be clearer cut, but the Web team might still want a healthy mixture of library clientele and supervisors.

Developing the target group is an important step and a crucial marketing tool if it's well thought out. After testing, many participants feel more included and have a better understanding of how the library interface is organized. If the final product is well done, the people who participated are happy to have been part of the process.

Following are some questions that will help narrow down your target group.

Who are your primary customers/clients/patrons?

Who do you feel really needs help navigating through your Web site?

Who can benefit from learning more about what the library is doing and the progress you are making with your Web site? (Examples might include library board members, school administrators, PTA members, department heads, or faculty members.)

Do you need to draw from a diverse demographic? (Examples might include Native Americans and the elderly.)

How many people overall do you need during multiple testing?

For example, a target group that might be appropriate for a public library could include

library board members

dedicated members over 55 (elderly)

reader advisory board

ethnically diverse customers

persons with disabilities

young adults (12–17)

adults (18+)

Friends of the library

Advertising

Once the Web team has an idea of the target group, it will have a better idea of where to advertise for participants. If the library is on a tight budget, the first place to advertise for usability testing participants is at the library itself on bulletin boards, in rest rooms, in study carrels, and beside computer terminals. You might also create an online advertisement on the library's home page; this will attract potential participants who are already familiar with the library interface and who access the library interface remotely. In addition, you could advertise at PTA meetings, at community service functions, in the campus newspaper, and in local community newspapers.

Before you advertise, you will want to determine whether you will offer incentives for participation. If so, what? At the University of Arizona, the participants were paid $10 to participate in the usability test. However, the University of Arizona Web team did not pay the participants if they were asked just a quick question. A rule of thumb is that if it will take more than thirty minutes to conduct the usability test, you will probably need some form of incentive for participants. For cases like these, librarians have used food, free printing cards, T-shirts, library book bags, etc., to entice participants.

If you are going to put advertisements in the library or on the library Web site, less information is better, otherwise many excellent participants might weed themselves out of the process for fear of the unknown. Leave the important information for the actual usability test. If the person presses for more information, provide it. The following advertisements (see figure 5.4) are brief, but the language will help get the maximum amount of callbacks.

FIGURE 5.4
Sample Advertisements to Recruit Participants

Would YOU like to make $10 helping out the library?

The library is currently recruiting participants of all ages.
Please contact the public service librarian, Elaina, if you are interested.
(555) 555-2742

Can you afford a few minutes to help the library?

The library is currently looking to recruit freshman and sophomore students.
Please contact the systems librarian, Jeff, if you are interested. (555) 555-9888

FREE $10 COPY CARDS to the first 10 people!

The first advertisement in figure 5.4 does not provide much information. It will be up to the contact person to screen out people. The overall goal of the advertisements is to get as many people interested as possible. This way the Web team has a better chance of getting the target group and not having to spend too much time continuously looking for participants.

TRAIN MODERATORS AND RECORDERS

Each participant is accompanied by a moderator and a recorder during the test. The Web team will need to determine who will be the moderator and who will be the recorder during each usability testing session. In some cases, everyone on the Web team will be given at least one chance to be both the moderator and the recorder. However, the recorder and moderator have very important but different roles that will help determine that test results are unbiased.

Moderators

Although some participants will feel right at home searching the computer and will not get frustrated, many others will be terrified and slightly uncomfortable about not being very computer savvy and making mistakes. With these latter participants, moderators may have a strong urge to "help" the participant find the right answer through direct suggestions or indirect body language. This does not help the Web team find out what the participant usually does when accessing the library interface in his or her natural environment. Moderators have a crucial role of making sure the person remains comfortable and provides meaningful and useful suggestions. In corporate and huge software companies, trained professionals who are comfortable communicating with a variety of people are the moderators who conduct multiple usability tests. These experienced moderators and consultants can conduct or train the Web team (for a large sum of money). However, the Web team should not have to hire a professional. Nevertheless, it is important that the moderator understands his or her role and takes it very seriously.

Moderators should be provided with the following description of their responsibilities:

1. Try not to become "too attached" to the Web site or uncomfortable if a participant makes a radical suggestion. This is particularly relevant for moderators who are Web masters, subject specialists, or someone who has worked on the creation of the Web site. Sometimes when a person puts a

tremendous amount of effort on a product, it's hard to accept criticism or watch participants make mistakes.

2. Keep body language neutral. Because the moderator is usually right next to the person doing the task, the participant will notice the moderator's body language. The participant can easily pick up on nonverbal signals and will look to the moderator for help.

3. Be encouraging and know when to calm down a frustrated and nervous participant. This goes back to using the script the Web team has written before conducting the test. If the participant voices being frustrated or says things like "I know I must look or seem stupid," the moderator must reassure the participant that the Web site, not the person, is the problem.

4. Keep the participant talking out loud. Talking out loud while searching a Web site is not a normal or natural behavior. Even though the moderator will stress talking out loud in the beginning, the participant may revert back to saying nothing. At this time it's important to ask "What are you thinking?" or "Tell me what you are thinking at this moment" to keep the person on track.

5. Be naturally inquisitive, and know when to prompt a participant for additional information. Sometimes the participant will give vague answers or limited information while searching the Web site. For example, if the person gets stuck on the catalog page, the moderator may ask, "What are you thinking here?" The person may simply respond: "This page is not well organized." As in a reference interview, the moderator needs to get to the root of why the site is not well organized.

6. Allow the participant to completely give up on a task before going to the next. There will be a great urge to help the participant when he or she gets lost or confused. Although a major part of a librarian's job responsibility is to help people access information, the moderator has to realize that if the person were accessing the library Web site remotely, he or she would not have a librarian to help. Let the person go through his or her natural search strategy even if the end result is giving up in frustration. Above all, the moderator has to remain neutral.

7. Do not suffocate the participant. Allow the person to breathe and feel comfortable. This is hard because the goal is to extract as much information from the participant as possible, but the moderator cannot crowd the person. The moderator sits next to the person but has to give the participant enough space to comfortably navigate around the computer. Moreover, do not hound the person with endless questions. Know when to hold back if the person feels pressured and perhaps save additional questions for after all the tasks or questions are completed.

8. Record the path. The recorder will have his or her hands full writing down everything the person says, so the moderator should record the path of pages or links the person clicks on before finding the right answer.

Recorders

Recorders also have some distinct responsibilities. The recorder writes down everything the participant says when thinking out loud and any important points the moderator makes during the testing. After the test, the moderator can give the recorder the path sheet, and the recorder should summarize the major points. The moderator and recorder should debrief each other on the test immediately after the participant leaves. Depending on which strategy is used to analyze the data, the recorder needs to put the information into the correct format. The recorder also has to remain neutral and not influence the study through nonverbal signals. The participant, if lost, will look to both the moderator and the recorder for a possible solution. The recorder can sit slightly behind the participant and the moderator. The recorder must also resist the urge to help the participant if he or she gets lost.

FIND THE RIGHT ROOM FOR TESTING

Finding the right room for testing is a major step to make sure the participant is comfortable. Do not schedule usability testing in the reference area or any other public place unless the testing consists of only approaching someone with a quick question. Because the person will need to talk out loud while the moderator and recorder watch every move, it will add an extra level of anxiousness if other people are wandering around the reference area.

Instead, use an office that will provide complete privacy. The office should be large enough to accommodate the moderator, recorder, and the participant without being cramped. Another area is a staff development training room or a room that has only a few computers and lots of space. The major component in finding the right room is for the participant to have enough privacy and lots of space to feel comfortable.

Consideration for Persons with Disabilities

Involving persons with disabilities creates an opportunity to explore ways to address their needs for effective and efficient access to information resources. Often many insights gained from including this group of users may be beneficially applicable to other user groups. The use of computer-based adaptive or assistive technologies allows persons with disabilities to participate in usability testing.

First, you will want to develop an action plan that includes an assessment of the computer-based adaptive equipment that is available onsite. Is an office or person assigned to provide services for persons with disabilities at your organization or institution? If so, make an appointment to discuss your desire to include persons with disabilities in your tests. Also ask for a demonstration of the adaptive computer equipment and discuss the issues involved in using it.

Next, you should know what types of disabilities can be reasonably accommodated in your usability testing environment. Persons with visual impairment, hearing impairment, and/or mobility challenges may be participants if the appropriate tools are available for assistance. However, keep in mind that persons with nonvisible or hidden disabilities should be considered too. These people may have psychological disabilities or learning disabilities such as dyslexia, for example.

Some accommodations will be much simpler to institute than others and will probably not require relocation of the testing site. For example, some of the physical mobility issues such as accommodating persons in a wheelchair may require only adjustable computer tables. The use of an ergonomically designed mouse with the tracking ball located on the top instead of on the bottom may be needed for those persons who do not have full motion or control of their hands. However, if a "sticky key" tool (used when more than one simultaneous key stroke is needed) is required for them to type, the test would have to be administered at the site where this equipment is located.

A broad selection of adaptive/assistive tools are available to accommodate persons with visual impairments. Text enlargement tools are probably the easiest to accommodate in the testing process. Remember that the print size on any paper materials used by participants should be larger than normal. "Drag and dictate" tools are useful to some persons with visual impairments, but remember that the skill level in using them can vary greatly from one person to another. Other tools such as the Kurzweil Reading Machine, closed captioning decoder, or other speech decoders may be too difficult to include without some expert assistance. The use of braille or a refreshable braille display are also not easy to accommodate in functional tests.

Accommodating persons with learning or psychological disabilities may involve simply allowing them more time to complete tasks. Sometimes offering them a variety or duplication of test materials in alternative media such as paper, flip chart, and verbal testing may suffice.

Including persons with disabilities in usability testing benefits the disabled by including their voices and views. These inclusions benefit the usability testing process by making sure it is influenced and shaped by the full spectrum of users that will use the interface being tested.

THE TEST

If time allows, the Web usability testing team have a trial run before actually testing so they can work out the kinks. The moderator and the recorder will want to make sure that they are asking the right questions within the correct time frame and are not leading the participant to biased conclusions. Enlist other library members in the trial run. If you are a solo librarian, maybe someone from the Web usability testing team or your supervisor can be the test subject for the trial run. Overall, working out the last-minute bugs will help the moderator and recorder feel more at ease and confident before the test. However, regardless of how much preparation the team does before bringing in the participants, sometimes the computers will start acting up or a participant may fail to show up. Make sure that you always have a backup contingency plan. Sometimes during testing you might have to enlist a participant who was not on the team's original list. Also have someone available to call on who has the technological expertise to troubleshoot any last-minute problems. For more information about the test itself, consult the hypothetical test in chapter 6.

ANALYZE THE RESULTS

Large corporations have been using quantitative techniques to analyze the usability test results for years. At these large corporations, they usually have enough money to hire professional usability experts to collect data, analyze the data, and write a comprehensive report. However, you, no doubt, will need to analyze the data without complicated quantitative techniques. If your library is interested in exploring a variety of ways to analyze usability data, please check out the additional readings for books and articles, which provide in-depth scientific methods for analyzing data.

The easiest way to analyze the data is to look for patterns. This is why it is so important for the moderator and recorder to write down the important findings immediately after the usability test. After the last test, the Web team can get together and compare the findings and make changes to the Web site. For example, suppose that after ten usability tests, seven people had problems finding the online catalog page because the term "online resources" did not make sense to them. After questioning participants about what term would be more helpful, two people remarked that it should just say "where to find books" and two others said you should use "online catalog." A way to handle this problem is to test both changes in another quick round of usability testing. The Web team can decide if they want a formal round of usability testing or just want to ask people in the library which term works best for them.

Many times there will be many comments and lots of suggestions. Some of the suggestions might not be technically feasible; others might be mentioned by only one or two people. It will be up to the expertise of the Web team to decide which patterns and suggestions need to be considered seriously. However, if the Web team notices something that is very obviously hindering participants from completing the tasks and questions, you should make those changes during the round of testing and then continue testing other participants. There is no need to keep testing something that obviously does not work.

Some Web teams will want to use more of a scientific analysis method for the usability testing involving a low-cost and low-stress method to gather statistical information. If the Web team created goals and objectives before they developed tasks and questions, they can use these objectives to analyze the data. For example, figure 5.5 shows the objective and items—together with a compilation of responses—that were first presented in figure 5.1.

Looking at this objective, 80 percent (or 8 people out of 10) is the acceptable number of correct responses for a successful library Web site. If the numbers are lower, the Web team needs to look over the comments and begin to make changes. The number in bold is the number of people (out of ten) who were able to successfully complete the task. From these results, the Web team

FIGURE 5.5
Sample Results of Academic Library Web Site Usability Test

Objective: When given various tasks, 80 percent of the participants will successfully be able to complete each task to locate books, articles, and journals while searching the library Web site.

Tasks

1. Find two books on capital punishment. (books) **9**
2. Find out if the journal *Educational Policy* is in the library. (journal titles) **5**
3. Find articles on business management. (articles) **5**
4. Find an article and a book on animal testing. (article and book) **5, 9**
5. If the above article is not full text, see if it is in the library. (journal title) **2**

---

could conclude that participants were comfortable finding books but not finding articles. The first task posed a problem for only one participant; therefore, the Web team might want to exclude this as a future usability task because the participants exceeded the goal. Instead, they could focus on another aspect of the Web site. However, it is important to determine why the one participant had trouble finding the book. For example, there may be another location to link that catalog page within the library interface. Remember, putting links in several places only increases the chance that more customers will be successful navigating the library Web site.

Looking at the results for item 2, it becomes apparent that half of the participants were confused about how to use a citation to find out if that material is located in the library. Furthermore, only two participants were able to successfully find out if an article is in the library (question 5). The Web team may have expected problems with this question since this task is a common academic reference desk question from undergraduate students. However, it is the Web team's responsibility to go over the comments and start developing strategies to make finding articles easier. Once the team has something in place, they should retest it. With the results in hand, the Web team has concrete numbers to show the rest of the library staff as they continue to test, modify, and retest the library interface.

Look at another example, shown in figure 5.6, for the results of testing presented in figure 5.2 for a public library.

FIGURE 5.6
Sample Results of Public Library Web Site Usability Test

Objective: When given various tasks, 70 percent of the participants will successfully be able to complete each task to locate books, videos, branch locations, and operating hours while searching the library Web site.

Tasks and Questions

1. Find a book on home gardening. (books using title or key word search) **8**
2. Find when the Dupont (western) branch closes on Wednesday. (branch hours) **7**
3. Do we have a branch named Manchaca? (branch) **6**
4. Find books by Maya Angelou. (books using author search) **5**
5. Does the library have any Jane Fonda videos? (videos) **3**
6. Find which library has the video "Get in Shape NOW" by Donna Richardson. (video and branch) **2**

Looking at the objective, 70 percent (or 7 people out of 10) is the public library's acceptable number of correct responses for a successful round of usability testing. The number in bold is the number of people (out of ten) who were able to successfully answer the question or complete the task. Items 1 and 2 were answered successfully by seven or more people. From these results, the Web team can conclude that the participants were able to find a book using the key word or title search. Looking at responses to items 5 and 6, you can see that participants had trouble limiting the basic key word to title searches to find videos. From the low scores, the Web team could work on making the branch information, author search, and the limit option more intuitive. After this change has been completed, the team would retest and hope the numbers fit the original objective.

Figure 5.7 shows the goal and items—together with a compilation of responses—that were presented in figure 5.3.

Items 2 and 3 stumped the majority of the school teachers. In this case, the Web team should look at the possibility of redesigning or reevaluating the location of the Web resources. Afterward, they could retest the two items again separately to see if the teachers are successfully able to complete the question or task.

FIGURE 5.7
Sample Results of School Library Web Site Usability Test

Objective: When given various tasks, 70 percent of the teachers will successfully be able to complete each task to find Web resources and specialized resources when searching the library Web site.

Tasks and Questions

1. Find the "Best School Reference Sites for Science Classes" on the Web page. (Web resources) **9**
2. Where does the library have information on creating online research modules? (Web resources) **4**
3. Find the "Join the Educational Discussion Group" on the Web site. Locate the discussion group that provides information about educationally relevant Internet resources. (Web resources) **2**
4. The library has a link to help you reserve books or articles for term papers and assignments. Find this link, and go through the process of reserving a book. (specialized resources) **8**
5. [directed to specific teachers] Find which Web resource packages were created for your classroom instruction. (Web resources) **8**

As the Web team continues to make changes and then conducts more usability tests, the overall results for the goals will improve over time. In this way you will have quantifiable numbers as the Web team continues to test and retest the library interface.

Applying the Results of the Testing for Solo Librarians

With the results of the testing in hand, how do you apply all the wonderful suggestions with a small staff and an even smaller budget? Some of the results are likely to refer to small changes to the Web site, such as changes of colors or font size, which are not mammoth tasks to complete. However, what about those suggestions to add unique graphics or revamp entire sections? One approach may be to request additional funding to outsource these tasks using the data obtained from the usability testing to justify the request. If the skill sets to accomplish these changes are available on staff, then targeted staff may be requested to work full-time to produce the modifications for some specified time period. Remember to include in these requests the resources needed to retest after the changes have been made.

Most interfaces are becoming graphic intensive because graphics provide an effective and attractive alternative to text-only navigation. Again, if the skills are available on staff to create the needed graphics, then request that person's time for the task. If the interface serves an academic environment, then perhaps students on campus could be recruited from the art department, for example, who may be interested in creating this work as part of an internship opportunity.

6

Usability Testing Example

The following usability test involves a fictitious library, Trihard University, to show how the process works. The interface for the Trihard University library was created after closely examining several library Web sites across the country. It includes some of the subtle and not so subtle design errors encountered when searching for a book or an article on many real library interfaces. The remainder of this chapter is written as a report of the fictitious Web team's activities. If your Web team just started with this chapter and some of the steps are unfamiliar, please take a look at the earlier chapters for more clarification.

OVERVIEW OF THE STEPS

Before our Web team got started with the actual usability test, it developed a detailed agenda of the process. This will help us remain focused and organized throughout the usability test, especially when conducting multiple tests. Below is our detailed outline showing the variety of steps involved in the beginning stages of usability testing.

form the Web team

establish goals and objectives

develop the questions and tasks

write the script

recruit participants

decide on a moderator and recorder

set up the room and coordinate times

test the test and work out kinks

give the test and record results and paths

analyze the data

make revisions to the Web site

retest

FORM THE WEB TEAM

The composition of the Web team brings together a combination of public service and technical service librarians and library staff members. The Web team also needs to have a person who has the authority to make changes to the library Web site. The dean and/or assistant dean will be ad hoc Web team members if necessary, but they will only participate in the usability testing as recorders. If possible, the Web team will solicit recorders to get buy-in from other library members about the importance of doing usability testing.

Here is the makeup of the Trihard Library Web team and our reasons for choosing these people:

technical services librarian (has authority to make changes)

information access librarian (has authority to make changes on the library interface and provides library instruction to our customers)

reference librarian (works directly with our customers and does some library instruction)

library student worker (gives us a student's perspective)

ad hoc members when available (such as the library dean or assistant dean)

ESTABLISH GOALS AND OBJECTIVES

The overall goal of the Trihard University library is to make the Web site more user-friendly to local and remote users. We know that most people access the library Web site in the dorms or off campus. In addition, Trihard University is setting up a distance education program, so we anticipate delivering more electronic resources and other services through the library interface in the future. The usability test will check to see if customers are able to find books, articles, and Web resources from the Trihard University library home page.

> **Goal:** To have a Web site at which customers can successfully find books and articles on their particular topic.

> **Objective:** To have students successfully find where our catalog and electronic databases are located and use them correctly at least 70 percent of the time during the usability testing process.

Note that we not only have an outcome but also a measure (70 percent). This will help us when we analyze the data. This goal is only specific to this particular test and might change slightly later. For example, next time we might be looking to see if customers can find electronic journals, interlibrary loan information, or the times the library is open.

DEVELOP THE QUESTIONS AND TASKS

We have tried to develop tasks and questions that relate directly to our goals and objectives. For this particular round of questioning, the goal is to see if students are able to find where the catalog and electronic databases are and to see if the directions or information we are providing them helps students know the difference between databases and the catalog. (See figure 6.1.)

FIGURE 6.1
Objective and Tasks for First Round of Testing

Objective: When given various tasks, 70 percent of students will successfully be able to complete each task while navigating through the library's Web site.

Tasks and Questions

1. Find a book on capital punishment. (book)
2. Find two articles about violence in music videos using the electronic resource EBSCOhost. Where would you get started? (articles)
3. Find an article from the journal *Topics in Education* v51, 1994. (locating journal titles in the library)
4. Find the book *I Know Why the Caged Bird Sings*. Is it currently checked out? (circulation records)
5. What two things worked well while searching the library interface?
6. What two things could be improved?

A print preassessment survey was distributed to the patrons over a four-week period.

The Web team learned that finding books, articles, and Web resources is confusing to most students.

The tasks involve a combination of looking in the catalog and looking in the electronic databases. Items 3 and 4 are fairly complex. Questions 5 and 6 will help us get feedback on the library Web site and clarify anything that really stood out as barriers for the student answering the question. This feedback will be crucial when debriefing and analyzing the results.

WRITE THE SCRIPT

Next, we developed a generic script. (See figure 6.2.) We gave each moderator a copy and left extras in the testing room and at the reference desk.

RECRUIT PARTICIPANTS

Now that various times and a location have been secured, we can recruit participants. The target market for this particular usability test is undergraduate students who either visit the library or access library resources off campus. We decided that graduate students might be more skilled in finding books and articles, but newer students would not be as used to the library interface. The enticement was $5 an hour. It could possibly go up to $10, but since there are only five questions, we figured that a better amount was $5 for this round. We placed advertisements in the library by the computer terminals, e-mail terminals, and study carrels and in the student union. An advertisement also went in the campus newspaper to get at the potential remote campus users. We had a few disgruntled students from the preassessment survey who were also included in the list of potential participants.

The advertisement was quick and simple. (See figure 6.3.) It was pretty vague because we were concerned that the more information provided, the less likely the student would follow through. When a potential student called the reference librarian, the librarian just scheduled the person for an appropriate time for testing. We wanted to test ten people; therefore, the reference librarian kept a waiting list of ten extra students in case someone canceled or did not show up.

FIGURE 6.2
Trihard University Library's Script

(At the entrance to the room)

Hello _____. Thank you for participating in our usability study!

My name is Lisa, and I am the reference librarian at Trihard University library. I will be asking you some questions today.

I don't know if the person on the phone or who responded to your e-mail told you about why you're here.

If not, we want to make sure the library Web site is usable and you are able to find information to help you with your research. Therefore, we will be asking you some questions, which you will answer by searching our Web site.

The whole study should not take any longer than 30 to 50 minutes.

(After the person enters the room)

The two people who will be in the room during the study will be the recorder and myself. The recorder will be writing down important points you bring up while searching the library Web site. To make sure we capture all your suggestions, we need you to talk out loud. More importantly, let us know when you're stuck or something does not make sense.

As you go through our test site, some of the links are not active, and we will clue you to stop searching or to move on to the next task.

Keep in mind that we are testing the library Web site, *not* you! If you find that something does not make sense or the answer is not obvious, this is the necessary information we need to make changes. Do you have any questions?

We will start by asking you a few demographic questions. Then we'll give you a chance to look at the Web site.

FIGURE 6.3
Trihard University's Advertisement for Participants

UNDERGRADUATE STUDENTS!

Want to make $5 for answering 5 questions?

If so call Lisa, reference librarian, at 555-1620.

DECIDE ON MODERATOR AND RECORDER

The information access librarian and the reference librarian decided to take turns as the moderator. Both people felt comfortable talking to students and are used to working with the public on a daily basis. They also felt at ease probing and remaining neutral from their experiences teaching and working at the reference desk. The technical services librarian, ad hoc members, and the library student worker will take turns as the recorders.

SET UP THE ROOM AND TIMES

The room we decided on was an office with plenty of space for three people (recorder, moderator, and participant). We could have used the electronic classroom, but it was too big and impersonal. The reference room has too many people wandering around, and the participant might become distracted or feel self-conscious. We also had to be flexible with testing times because many students have hectic schedules. To account for this, we coordinated times where at least two people could be available for a certain hour, but we left plenty of time available in case someone needed to meet after 5:00.

TEST THE TEST

This is Trihard University's first usability test, so we have asked a few library staff members to participate in mock testing. We want to make sure that the moderators and recorders remain neutral throughout the usability test and that they start feeling comfortable with the generic script.

GIVE THE TEST AND RECORD RESULTS AND PATHS

Now that all the things are in place, we have completed ten rounds of usability testing. For each round of testing, the moderator wrote down the path and the recorder wrote down everything the person said. Immediately after the test, the recorder and moderator for that particular round of testing wrote down the major points they both learned. The summary in figure 6.4 was written up immediately after the moderator and recorder got together and agreed on what happened during the test.

FIGURE 6.4
Summary of One Round of Testing

Moderator: reference librarian

Recorder: library student

Participant's name: Tracy Johns

Status: sophomore

Major: psychology

Familiarity with Internet: searches it every day

Use of library Web site: once a month

1. Find a book on capital punishment.

   She found the book but had some problems. Clicked on several of our "under construction" pages before she found the catalog. Thought the catalog was hard to use with too many inner pages. A suggestion is to eliminate some of the wording on the catalog page.

2. Find two articles about violence in music videos using EBSCOhost. Where would you get started?

   Never found EBSCOhost. Gave up in frustration after clicking and finding the catalog three times. Thought that the catalog was the way to find EBSCOhost. Did not understand how to get started finding the articles. Suggestion: Home page should state "Where to Find Articles."

3. Find an article from the journal *Topics in Education* v51, 1994.

   Did not answer this question. Did not know where to start or misunderstood the concept of when to go to the catalog and when to search databases. Suggestion: Have a help link for people who need it.

4. Find the book *I Know Why the Caged Bird Sings*. Is it currently checked out?

   Did get this one because she had already found the catalog page from the previous question and the circulation information is on that page.

5. What two things worked well while searching the library interface?

   Colors/graphics are nice.
   Front page is visually pleasing.

6. What two things could be improved?

   Make words more obvious, such as "catalog" and "articles."
   Get rid of "under construction" page.

The following screen shots further illustrate some of the suggestions the participants pointed out during the usability tests.

A.

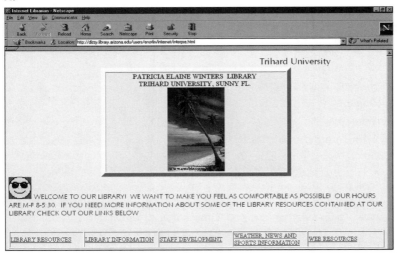

All participants started with the library's home page, shown in screen shot A. Taking a look at this Web page, some participants did not understand the difference between "library resources" and "library information." They also were not clear about exactly what might be found under "Web resources" or about the amount or detail of the information. What was very clear was that for our first usability test question, it was not clear where the catalog page was or which box to choose first.

B.

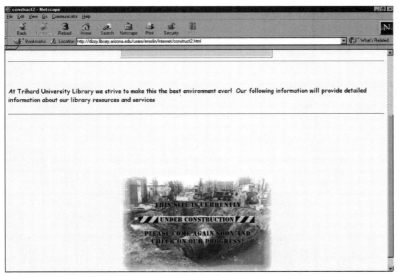

Web page B shows what the participant got after clicking on a page that is under construction.

C.

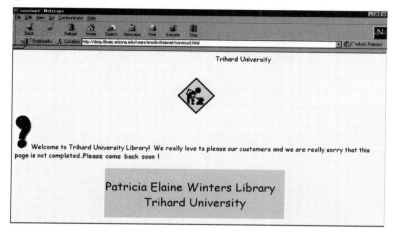

Screen shot C shows the Web page the participant got after clicking on "library resources." It also is under construction.

D.

The catalog page is under "library information." When the participant clicked on "library information," screen shot D is what they initially saw. Notice that the online catalog page is not visible. The online catalog link is actually at the bottom of the page.

E.

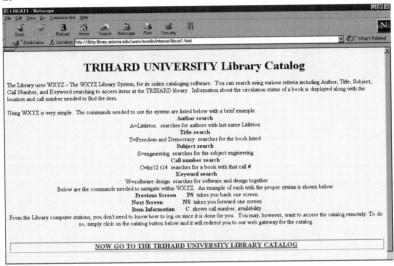

The participant had to scroll down to the bottom of the page to find the link to the online catalog page. (Shown in screen shot E.)

F.

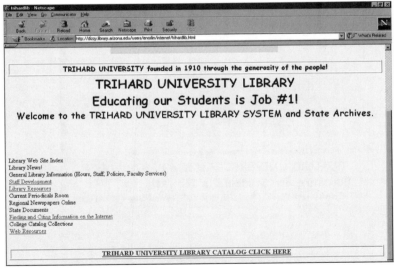

After the participant scrolled to the bottom of the page and clicked on the online catalog page, this extra page (screen shot F) was introduced with another link to click on at the bottom. This Web page was designed to give students an opportunity to learn how to search the catalog. However, most participants were lost.

G.

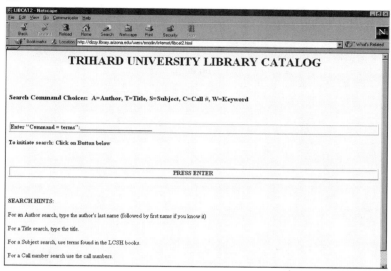

After four clicks and scrolling to the bottom of pages, the participant finally discovered where to start his or her search for the questions about finding a book or journal title in the catalog. (See screen shot G.)

H.

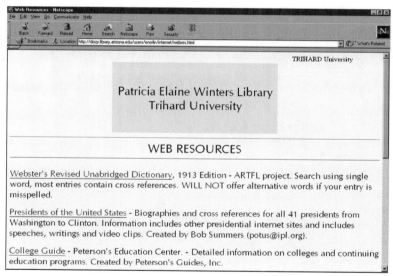

Another difficult task was to find EBSCOhost. EBSCOhost is located within the Web resources page. Screen shot H shows what the participant saw after clicking on the original link. Notice that there was no obvious link to EBSCOhost on the first page.

I.

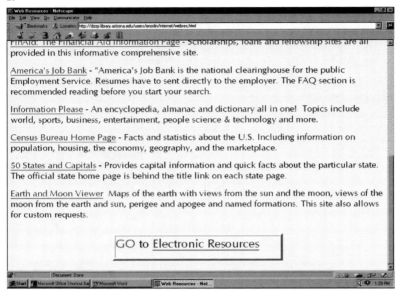

Actually there is a link to "electronic resources" at the bottom of the page. (See screen shot I.) Some participants were not sure if this would really lead to EBSCOhost. EBSCOhost is an electronic resource.

J.

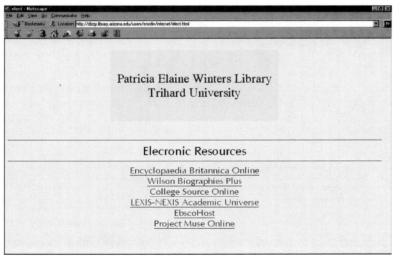

After three clicks, participants found EBSCOhost. (See screen shot J.)

ANALYZE THE DATA

After the ten rounds of testing, we listed the number of people who actually completed the task. (See figure 6.5.)

The usability test was not successful for any of the tasks. We did get some valuable feedback on where to get started in modifying the library interface. After being momentarily depressed about the low numbers, we started to look at the feedback. The last two questions and the suggestions were very helpful. Most participants, especially the ones who were not successful, had the following tips:

Make words more obvious, such as "catalog" and "articles"

Get rid of "under construction" page

Too wordy

Under construction pages were very confusing

Need to get to the catalog and articles with less clicks

Catalog page takes too many clicks to reach

Add more words in some sections to make things clearer

What's the difference between library information and library resources?

Do not understand what is contained in "Web resources"

Can't the articles and books be linked on the same page?

Need help pages

Do not put the link to catalog page at the bottom

Too much scrolling; things need to be centralized

FIGURE 6.5
Tabulation of Results

1. Find a book on capital punishment. (book) **4**

2. Find two articles about violence in music videos using EBSCOhost. Where would you get started? (articles) **2**

3. Find an article from the journal *Topics in Education* v51, 1994. (locating journal titles in the library) **1**

4. Find the book *I Know Why the Caged Bird Sings.* Is the book currently checked out? (circulation records) **4**

MAKE REVISIONS TO THE WEB SITE

After reviewing the comments and reexamining the Trihard University library's Web pages, we decided to make some changes. The technical services librarian, along with the Web team's input and input from other library staff members, completely redesigned some of the Web pages. The main emphases of the changes were

- making the online catalog page quicker to get to and more obvious
- separating the Web resources from the electronic resources
- eliminating the tasks that call for links to "under construction" pages
- making the wording less ambiguous
- providing links to the online catalog and electronic databases at more than one location

The following screen shots show what the Trihard University library interface looks like after modification.

K.

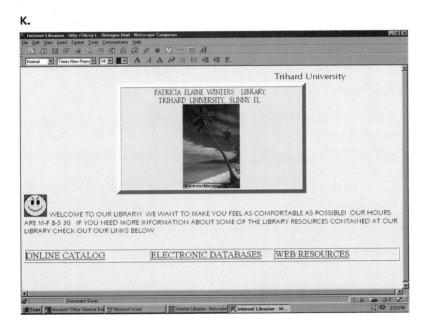

The links on the home page (screen shot K) have been changed to three from five. The online catalog is now a link on the home page. The link "electronic databases" is used to help students find EBSCOhost.

L.

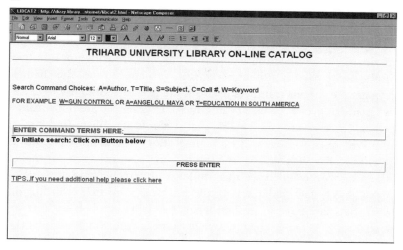

With the revision, the participant can start searching in the online catalog after one click. Screen shot L shows the search page. If the participant needs additional help, a tip line at the bottom of the page leads to additional information.

M.

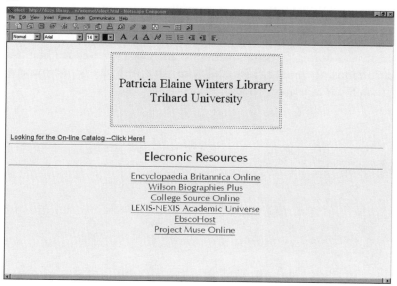

From the home page the database EBSCOhost can also be found after one click. (See screen shot M.)

RETEST

The new Trihard University library interface will not go up until we retest the changes. The library interface is not completed because the hours, location, interlibrary loan, staff phone numbers, and e-mail, etc., information is not yet located on the home page and the inner pages. We want to retest the changes and work to get the success numbers up from the previous usability test. The changes we made improve the library interface. However, we are not finished with our work. Once we are comfortable that students are able to find books, articles, and Web resources, we will start integrating general information. As we slowly redesign the Web site, we will test the progression to see if it makes sense to the users. We want to see that students understand and are able to navigate through our new changes. Will students need some extra wording on the electronic database page to explain what they will get when clicking on electronic resources? We will retest that page to make sure. We plan to let the users know on the library home page that the library is starting to make changes to the Web site. We will ask customers to let us know what they think of the changes. Through this avenue we will continue to recruit participants for future usability testing and to work out conflicts and concerns we have about our approach.

Web site usability testing need not be complicated. In this book, we have presented the more practical guidelines to Web site usability testing. This process will be of great use to library-based Web developers and designers who need a cost-effective, customer-centered method of analysis. However, reading this book and infrequently testing the usability of your Web site is not enough. After all, usability is as usability does.

Additional Readings

Creswell, J. W. 1994. *Research Design: Qualitative and Quantitative Approaches.* Thousand Oaks, Calif.: Sage.

del Galdo, E. M., and J. Nielsen, eds. 1996. *International User Interfaces.* New York: Wiley.

Dumas, Joseph. 1993. *A Practical Guide to Usability Testing.* Norwood, N.J.: Ablex.

Forsythe, Chris. 1998. *Human Factors and Web Development.* Mahwah, N.J.: Lawrence Erlbaum Associates.

Garlock, K. L., and S. Piontek. 1999. *Designing Web Interfaces to Library Services and Resources.* Chicago: American Library Assn.

Gogolin, L., and F. Swartz. 1992. "A Quantitative and Qualitative Inquiry into the Attitudes toward Science of Nonscience College Students." *Journal of Research in Science Teaching* 29 (5): 487–504.

Howlett, V. 1996. *Visual Interface Design for Windows: Effective User Interfaces for Windows 95, Windows NT, and Windows 3.1.* New York: Wiley.

Mandel, Theo. (1997) *The Elements of User Interface Design.* New York: Wiley.

Norlin, E., and others. 1997. The Final Word: Why Do User Centered Evaluation? Available: http://dizzy.library.arizona.edu/library/teams/access9798/asu/ald025.htm.

Payette, S. D., and O. Y. Riger. 1998. "Supporting Scholarly Inquiry: Incorporating Users in the Design of the Digital Library." *Journal of Academic Librarianship* n.v.: 121–9.

Radosevich, L. 1997. "Fixing Website Usability." *InfoWorld* 19 (50): 81–2.

Rousseau, G. K., and others. 1998. "Assessing the Usability of Online Library System." *Behaviour and Information Technologies* 17 (5): 274–81.

Rubin, Jeffrey. 1994. *Handbook of Usability Testing: How to Plan, Design and Conduct Effective Tests.* New York: Wiley.

Smith, Wanda J. 1996. *ISO and ANSI Ergonomic Standards for Computer Products: A Guide to Implementation and Compliance.* Upper Saddle River, N.J.: Prentice-Hall.

Spool, Jared M. 1999. *Web Site Usability: A Designer's Guide.* San Francisco: Morgan Kaufmann.

Stempe, D. M., and E. M. Reingold. 1995. "Selection by Looking: A Novel Computer Interface and Its Application to Psychological Research." In *Eye Movement Research*, edited by M. Findley and others. Amsterdam: Elsevier.

INDEX

Elaina Norlin is the undergraduate librarian at the University of Arizona in Tucson. Her research interests include marketing in academic libraries, data analysis, multimedia technology, and library outreach. She is a published author with local, national, and international conference presentation experience, which includes Computers in Libraries, Internet Librarian, Minority University Space Interdisciplinary Network and Internet Librarian International. Norlin was project team member of Access 2000, a team that redesigned the University of Arizona's Web site through usability testing. She has delivered four local and national presentations on using usability testing efficiently, effectively, and inexpensively. Norlin received a Masters of Science degree in library and information science from the University of Illinois at Urbana-Champaign.

CM! Winters is a doctoral student at Florida State University's School of Information Studies where she is researching the historical role of the academic library in the institutional accreditation process and developing a conceptual framework to explain its effect on the development of African American colleges and universities. Her minor is in educational foundations and policy studies. Winters's additional interests are in academic library administration and the use of Web-based technology in bibliographic instruction.

Winters has participated in the University of Illinois at Chicago's library resident program after receiving a Masters of Science degree in library and information science from the University of Illinois at Urbana-Champaign and a bachelor's degree from De Paul University. She is a published author with professional conference experience and was recently selected to be part of the Gates Foundation's inaugural group of the Gates Millennium Scholars Program.